ideals
CHRISTMAS

Sing hey! Sing hey!
for Christmas Day;
twine mistletoe and holly,
for friendship glows
in winter snows,
and so let's all be jolly.
—Author Unknown

Nashville, Tennessee

Snow Fun
Lois Anne Williams

Snow is swirling through the air,
blowing, drifting everywhere.
Here come children dressed
    so warm,
happy with the first snowstorm.

With cheeks so rosy, hearts
    so gay,
they run to join their friends
    in play.

What can give them such a thrill
as a sled ride down the hill?

The trek back up is quite a chore
but must be done if they
    want more.
So up they march and form
    a line,
then off upon their swift decline.

New Friend
Virginia Blanck Moore

We've got a new friend
I'm delighted to say,
a brand-new companion
to help in our play.

He came just this morning
when snow fell at dawn
and spread, moist and lovely,
across the whole lawn.

We looked out the window,
and somebody cried,

"It's perfect for snow men—
quick! Run outside!"

We got booted and mittened,
and outdoors we flew.
And from three little snowballs,
how fast our friend grew!

Now he stands glistening;
our eyes with pride glow.
For we think he's just splendid—
our friend made of snow.

Image © Hazel Lincoln/Advocate Art

*Heap on more wood!—
the wind is chill;
but let it whistle as it will,
we'll keep our Christmas merry still.*
—Sir Walter Scott

Favorite Place
June Masters Bacher

Though riches allure us
and other lands call;
now isn't a fireside
the best place of all?

*Christmas is the season for kindling
the fire of hospitality in the hall,
the genial flame of charity in the heart.*
—Washington Irving

Fireside
Marguerite Kingman

The kitten purrs;
the kettle sings.
The heart remembers
little things.

The fire burns low;
the embers sigh . . .
We dream and doze—
the cat and I.

Image © Colin Poole/GAP Interiors

The Fireplace at Christmas

Andrew L. Luna

There is something very special about having a fireplace during the Christmas season. The warmth and light emitting from the burning logs seem to accentuate the radiance of the holidays and symbolize the special warmth that rests in the hearts of most during this sacred time of year.

Since the dawn of time, fire has served to melt the chill within our bones, make fresh kill or catch more palatable to the mouth, harden hand-formed clay, and ward off vicious creatures with its bright, flickering light. In modern times, fire serves more intangible needs: It bonds families together around its hearth, becomes a favorite companion to book and beverage, and quickly turns a comfortable room into a quiet, romantic getaway.

More importantly, however, a cozy fire causes us to stop for a while and ponder. As the flickering flames lap up the fuel from the logs and the red-hot embers hiss and crackle indiscriminately underneath, we find time to contemplate the long, hard day behind us and prepare for the future that waits. This is the perfect frame of mind to be in during Christmastime, when we take time to ponder our existence in relation to God's perfect gift to mankind.

As a boy, I loved a fire in the fireplace during Christmastime. I remember our creche was always placed to the left side of the hearth. While rearranging the cows, sheep, camels, and wise men around the manger, I imagined our fire was there to warm them all on that cold winter's night.

But the fire was not the sole component of warmth and cheer around that fireplace of ours. Mom always had the mantel decked out in its special holiday dress. Some years would see colored lights and garland gently draped over it. During others, there would be candles aflame next to strategically placed angel hair and Christmas balls borrowed from the tree. No matter how it was decorated, our mantel always joyously welcomed the season. To this day, I remember the mantel decorations twinkling in Dad's eye as he gazed at them and told Mom how cheery they were.

Now, the mantel was never over-decorated. After all, it had to support some of the most important items of the season: Christmas stockings. My sister and I usually had two stockings for all of the fruit, nuts, and candy that were left for us. To this day, an orange or tangerine pleasantly takes me back to my childhood and Christmas morning. For Mom and Dad's stocking, we used two stockings sewn together and made into a pair of Christmas pants. We even had stockings for our pet cats. To say our mantel was an exhibition during Christmas would be an understatement.

A fire in the fireplace at Christmastime rekindles my memories of hot chocolate and popcorn, nuts freshly cracked and hulls thrown into the fire for added fuel. I'm reminded of Christmas movies watched in flannel pajamas, curled up next to my dad in his chair, of our cats lazily sleeping while Mom worked in the kitchen baking her famous fruitcake cookies (which were always softer and more delectable than the actual cake from whence they got their name). I especially remember my job of going outside in the cold, frosty air to get fresh logs, only to be entranced by the warm, rich, acrid smell of woodsmoke from our chimney.

When we visited my aunt's house in Florence, Alabama, there would always be a crackling fire waiting for us in the living room. With the heat of so many people exchanging gifts, we would often allow the fire to almost completely extinguish itself. After the gifts had been given and the clutter had been cleared, the adults would drop colorful wrapping paper into the fire. We gazed in awe as the ink from the paper created flames of red, purple, yellow, and green.

As I grew older, the Christmas fireplace never lost its charm. I asked my wife to marry me in my parent's basement, romantically lit by Christmas tree and firelight. My family now has its own traditions of decorating the mantel and hanging stockings. But I still find solitude and comfort sitting by the fire with a Christmas story or gazing at the bright, colored lights on our tree.

Today the need for a real fireplace has been replaced by central heat and gas logs. While utilitarian in comfort and convenience, these do little to compare with a real crackling fire in a fireplace at Christmastime; the sight of which takes me back to simpler times and happy memories.

Image © Daniel Rodgers/Advocate Art

The Snow
Emily Dickinson

It sifts from leaden sieves,
It powders all the wood,
It fills with alabaster wool
The wrinkles of the road.

It makes an even face
Of mountain and of plain—
Unbroken forehead
    from the east
Unto the east again.

It reaches to the fence,
It wraps it, rail by rail,
Till it is lost in fleeces;
It flings a crystal veil

On stump and stack and stem—
The summer's empty room,
Acres of seams where
    harvests were,
Recordless, but for them.

It ruffles wrists of posts,
As ankles of a queen—
Then stills its artisans
    like ghosts,
Denying they have been.

Image © sphraner/Adobe Stock

December's Visitor
Eileen Spinelli

Christmas
comes calling
with pageants and wings,
with ribbons and holly
and popcorn on strings,
with boxes of tinsel,
with chestnuts and pies.
Christmas comes calling
with joy in her eyes.

Christmas
comes calling
with carols and bells,
with sparkling trees
and gingerbread smells,
with snowflakes and starlight
through cities and farms.
Christmas comes calling
with peace in her arms.

Christmas Eve
Loretta Bauer Buckley

Holly wreath and mistletoe,
bayberry candle, drifting snow;
happiness and warmth and light,
boundless love this joyous night;
stockings hanging in a row,
eyes alight, hearts aglow;
softly spoken words of prayer,
dreams of starlight everywhere!

Image © Natalia Greeske/Adobe Stock

The True Spirit of Christmas

Ruth C. Wintle

Caught up in the excitement and anticipation of Christmas, my six-year-old granddaughter, Karen, began making a long list of all the presents she hoped to find under the tree with her name on them that year.

Following a Sunday school lesson, her whole attitude changed. Her teacher read the story of the first Christmas and explained that the Heavenly Father sent His most precious possession, the Christ Child, as His unselfish gift of love to the world.

From that time on Karen began to understand that giving, not getting, was the miracle of Christmas. What could she give to others? She was short on money, but somehow she didn't think that gifts of love were bought at the store. Rather they came from the heart.

After much soul-searching, the answer came. She must give her cherished possessions. Carefully she wrapped her costume jewelry, her broken crayons, her storybooks, and other trinkets. She chose something for everyone on her list, until her small hoard of treasures was nearly exhausted.

Christmas morning, Karen, her face aglow with love, watched with rapt attention as we opened our gifts from her heart.

Amid the ribbon and wrappings of my package lay her favorite doll, a mischievous, freckle-face urchin with an impish wink and a bad haircut. Her genuine love for me, evidenced by her treasured gift, touched the center of my emotions. My first thought was: I can't take the doll that's so much a part of her childhood, her friend who shares her joys, sorrows, and all her secrets. It goes everywhere—even to bed—with her. Keeping it would be comparable to the villain in the melodrama who takes the baby for the mortgage payment.

On the other hand, no matter what explanations I might offer for refusing her priceless gift, she would feel it was unacceptable. In essence, it would be the same as Christ refusing the gifts of the Wise Men, which were no more precious. I had to keep it. I hugged her close, knowing I could never love her more than I did at the moment.

Karen is all grown up now, but my eyes still mist each time I look at the doll that occupies a place of honor among my treasures and remember a six-year-old child who showed me the true spirit of Christmas.

Image © k2photostudio/Adobe Stock

No Magazine Tree for Me!

Anne Kennedy Brady

One year, my mother almost ruined Christmas. I was in fourth grade, and we were discussing a date for putting up the Christmas tree. Each year we set aside an entire Saturday to decorate the house and the tree as a family. It was my favorite tradition. I loved riffling through ornaments from years past and reminiscing together. The satin animals Mom and Dad bought overseas pre-kids, the macaroni bell from my oldest brother's preschool year, a be-glittered bear I made in second grade—everything had a story. But this year, Mom threw a wrench in our perfectly holly-jolly works.

"How about this year, we just do red and silver on the tree?" she chirped.

Silence descended upon the dinner table.

"Like, just red and silver ornaments?" Doug asked. At four years older than me, he was almost too cool for family Christmas decorating, but not quite.

"Sure!" Mom replied. "Velvet bows and silver icicles, a few candy canes—it would be really beautiful. I saw it in a magazine."

I gasped. "What about the other ornaments?" I asked.

When she revealed that they would simply lay dormant in the garage for another year (at least!), the rest of the family took up my cause with passion, and Mom's proposal was vehemently voted down. At least that's how I remember it. It's possible things went down in a more civil manner, but I recall being absolutely horrified. Leave the ornaments in boxes? Never! They were practically members of the family!

Our Christmas tree sported its usual haphazard assortment of ornaments that year, macaroni bell and all. And I think Mom felt bad about the whole ordeal, because the following year she started a new tradition. Each December 1st, she said, she would give me a special ornament, so that by the time I had my own home, I would also have my very own collection to take with me.

That first year it was a hand-painted Nativity scene she'd picked up at the church craft fair. Other years, she took cues from significant events that had occurred in the previous twelve months. One year she took me to see a touring production of the musical CATS, and on December 1st, she gifted me a glass kitten ornament. The year I graduated high school, I received an angel sporting my school colors. I have ornaments commemorating my first job, milestone birthdays, family vacations, book releases, my wedding, and both of my kids' first Christmases. Every December 1st, I still look forward to opening the ornament Mom has tucked away for me, eager to relive a shared memory, despite the miles that now separate us.

My husband, Kevin, added his own collection to mine when we brought home our first Christmas tree—including more cartoon characters than one might expect—and therefore, it will come as no surprise that my own Christmas tree will never make the cover of a magazine. The branches slope awkwardly with the uneven weight of a clay rooster here or a popsicle sled there, and we couldn't be happier about it. With our kids at ages five and eight, I had been thinking about continuing my mom's tradition with them sometime soon. But Kevin beat me to the punch.

We usually take our children shopping to choose a gift for each other. This year, Kevin added an ornament to their task. The results were a delight. For Helen, Milo selected a bright pink car, emblazoned with a particular doll brand beloved by little sisters everywhere. Helen chose her older brother's ornament from a mall kiosk that offered written personalization on an enormous variety of scenes. On Christmas morning, he tore open the box to reveal a small ceramic child holding a box of French fries and shouting the name of Milo's favorite video game. Both kids could not have been more thrilled. They hung their ornaments as high as they could (for safety), and Milo told me several times, "I can't believe Helen got that for me."

My favorite trees will always be those with

Image © David Giles/GAP Interiors

no themes other than memories. Here is that year we visited Hawaii. There is the year we moved to Chicago. See the ballerina missing a finger? How about the faded photo of your cousin? Remember when Helen chose that for you? Remember when Milo gave you this one? These moments allow us to gather, to remember, and to celebrate the most important gift of Christmas: family. So, you can keep your velvet bows, your tasteful icicles, and your subdued color schemes. (And please do, if they bring joy to you and yours!) As for me, I'll be researching self-storage units, because I have a feeling this ornament tradition is going to stick around.

Little Lights
J. Harold Gwynne

Somehow the little colored lights
    are brighter than the rest;
of all the lovely Christmas sights,
    the little lights are best.

The rows and strings of lights we see
    are imaged on the snow;
but little lights upon the trees
    shine forth with mystic glow.

They shine like jewels rich and rare,
    in red, and blue, and green;
they look like flowers, bright and fair,
    that summer days have seen.

Perhaps the little lights are blessed
    with healing, light and mild,
because they burn and shine their best
    for Mary's little Child.

Legacy
Eileen Burnett

I saw Christmas.
'Twas a shining light,
not from a star
deep in the night,
not from a planet
far in the skies.
The light I beheld was
in a little girl's eyes.
So as she gazed at
the candles and tree,
the faith that is
Christmas
was kindled in me!

Image © JP Danko/Stocksy

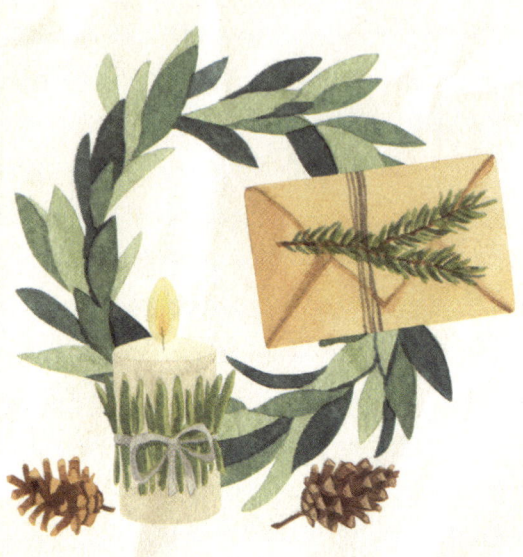

Christmas Cards

Rebekah Moredock

Envelopes are towering high—
let's open them and see
what friends and family have to say
in cards addressed to me.

Someone's babe has just been born;
a dear son's moved away.
Sally's daughter married Tom,
and George is home to stay.

Cards and smiling photos
tumble gently 'cross my lap,
such tangible reminders of
the joy of this year past.

For Christmas is a time
to reconnect with those you love,
with festive cards and letters
sharing blessings from above.

Image © Roy LANGSTAFF/Alamy Stock Photo

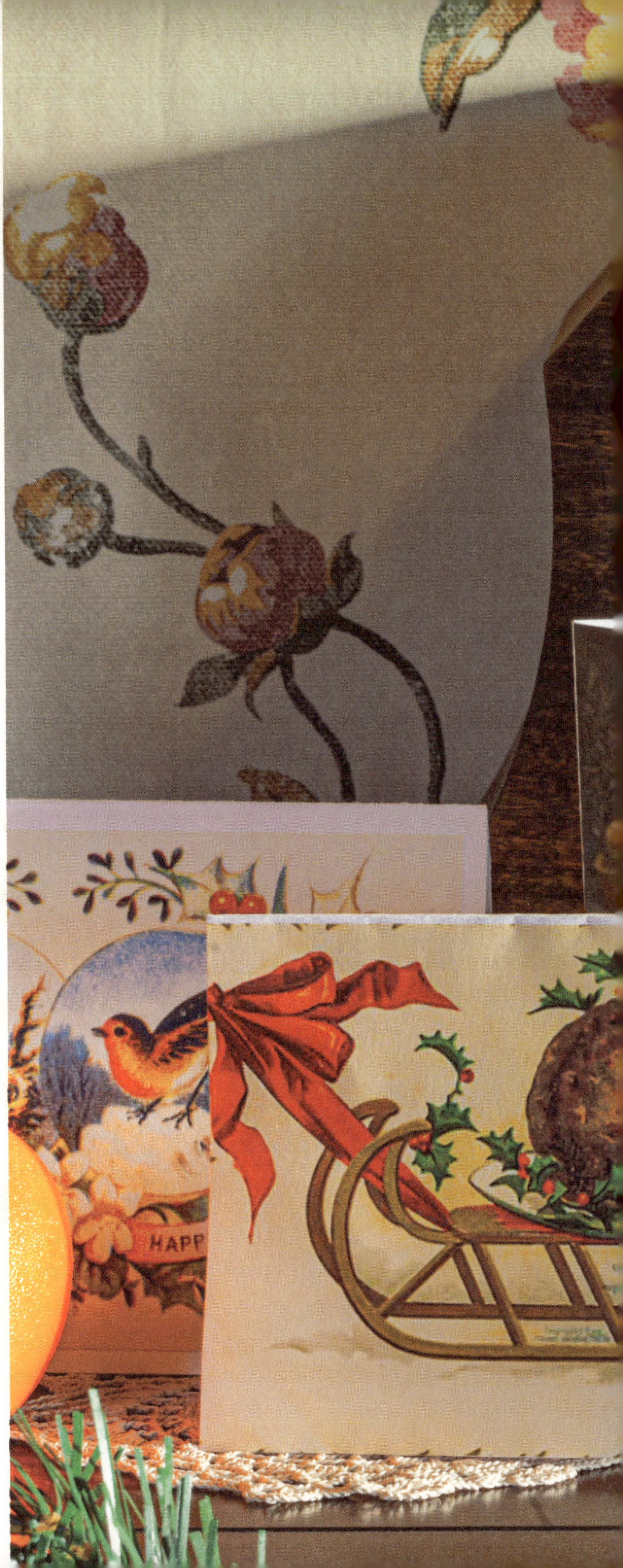

Christmas Is a Season for Giving
Helen Steiner Rice

Christmas is a season
    for gifts of every kind,
All the glittering, pretty things
    that Christmas shoppers find—
Baubles, beads, and bangles
    of silver and of gold—
Anything and everything
    that can be bought or sold
Is given at this season
    to place beneath the tree

For Christmas is a special time
    for giving lavishly.
But there's one rare and priceless gift
    that can't be sold or bought,
It's something poor or rich can give
    for it's a loving thought—
And loving thoughts are something
    for which no one can pay
And only loving hearts can give
    this priceless gift away.

Christmas Is for Cousins
Deborah A. Bennett

Christmas is for cousins
who are happy at your door
to see you, though it's been a while—
a week, or month, or more.

Christmas is for cousins
who are never quite the same,
but share adventures—
    secrets too—
and favorite songs and games.

Christmas is for cousins
who are sleeping on your floor,
who whisper with you every night,
and giggle til they snore.

Christmas is for cousins
who like you as you are,
and feel like friends when
    they are near—
like friends when they are far.

Last Minute Shopper © John Sloane. Used by permission. www.johnsloaneart.com

Image © steve bly/Alamy Stock Photo

A Farm-Fresh Christmas

Tracy Crump

Our son, Brian, was three when we moved from the big city to a country setting. We'd built a house in a large subdivision perched in the middle of farmland, and at night cows mooed in the fields behind us while barred owls called to their mates. Brian delighted in watching wild fox, deer, and rabbits venture forth from wooded areas on the undeveloped lots around our home. Though the city was not far away, breathing fresh, clean air invigorated us, and we enjoyed pretending to be bona fide country folk. Before long, another son, Jeremy, joined our family, and we settled in.

When Christmas rolled around, I dreamed of hiking across our own land to find the perfect tree, just as the early pioneers had. Sadly, with only a two-thirds-acre lot, we didn't have much land to hike across. So that December and for several thereafter, we continued our annual tradition of visiting the seasonal Christmas tree displays that graced vacant parking lots. We would still have a live tree, even if it had been cut weeks before and hauled in on a flatbed. After scouring the pickings, we chose the freshest one with the most even branches, shook out as many dead needles as possible, and took it home.

Then one year, we learned about the Merry Christmas Tree Farm that had recently opened. Not far from our house, it sported acres and acres of live evergreens just waiting to adorn homes during the holiday season. The boys shouted with delight when they learned they would get to cut their very own Christmas tree.

Our visit to the farm commenced with a ride in a wooden trailer pulled behind a tractor. My husband and I helped the boys, bundled in their heavy coats, onto hay bales lining the wooden platform. Off we went, jostling and bumping along trails and over a rickety bridge.

We finally reached a stand of Leyland cypress, and everyone got out. Growing in long rows spaced evenly apart, hundreds of trees stood straight and true in the red clay soil.

Branches had been trimmed here and there during their short lives to encourage thick, even growth. When we found the one we wanted—only about five feet tall but full and beautifully shaped—we stopped and signaled the farm employee.

After telling us the price, he bent to cut the tree, but my husband raised his bow saw. "Thanks, but we'll take care of it."

Brian and Jeremy lay on the ground on either side of the tree, their noses close to the fragrant needles, and began sawing back and forth. Even with the small trunk, it took young hands a while to make headway, but in time, the tree began to wobble. Triumphant, they finished the job, and we boarded the trailer with our prize to ride to the log cabin that served as an office.

The boys beamed as workers set the tree—*their* tree—on a homemade vibrator to shake off dead needles. They then ran it through a "wrapping" machine that pinned wayward branches snugly to its side with plastic mesh. Once paid for and strapped into the trunk, our little tree rode home to spend Christmas with us.

We hung a hodgepodge of ornaments—some made by the boys at school, some fashioned from gold- and silver-sprayed pinecones and gumballs tied with bright ribbon—on its branches. A quilted skirt my sister had made wrapped its trunk. Strings of colored lights heated the needles and released a piney scent. Never had our house smelled so evergreen and good.

Visiting the Merry Christmas Tree Farm became our new annual tradition. Decorating for Christmas became more special to the boys after that day because they'd cut the tree themselves. And I got to enjoy a farm-fresh Christmas in our cozy "country" home.

Christmas Cookie Magic
Louise Pugh Corder

There is in childhood's treasure chest
a custom I remember best—
the special, yearly family treat
when we baked Christmas
    cookies sweet.
An expert cook, Mom cast her spell.
Her students stirred and sifted well.
The room became a magic place;
we watched Mom mix and
    knead with grace.
Then every child, bright eyes aglow,
rolled out a precious bit of dough
and cut out chosen shapes with care
in spicy, fragrant Christmas air.
As cookies into oven went,
our mouths all watered at the scent—
till out they came, a welcome sight,
quite golden brown and baked
    just right.
Each one of us would sample one
the very minute they were done
and frost the Santa, Christmas tree,
bell, star, and reindeer shapes with glee.
In modern kitchen, I recall
our cookie fun when I was small,
get out Mom's favorite recipes,
and plan to make some memories.

Image © egal/iStock

Family Recipes

Breakfast Sausage Bake

20	ounces shredded hash browns, thawed	8	eggs
1	pound ground pork sausage	2	teaspoons Dijon mustard, optional
½	medium onion, finely chopped	½	teaspoon salt
½	red pepper, diced	¼	teaspoon black pepper
½	green pepper, diced	¼	teaspoon cayenne pepper, optional
1½	cups milk	2	cups shredded cheddar cheese

Preheat the oven to 350°F. Grease a 9 x 13-inch baking dish and spread hash browns in a layer. Set aside.

In a large skillet over medium-high heat, cook sausage, breaking up into small pieces, until no pink remains. Drain excess fat. Add onion and peppers; cook until vegetables begin to soften. Layer sausage mixture over hash browns. In a large bowl, whisk together milk, eggs, mustard, salt, and peppers. Pour egg mixture over hashbrown and sausage; mix gently. Sprinkle cheese on top. Bake uncovered for 50 to 60 minutes until edges are beginning to brown and center is set. If top is browning too quickly, loosely cover with foil for last 10–15 minutes. Let stand for 5 minutes before serving. Makes 8 to 10 servings.

Orange-Cranberry Scones

6	tablespoons granulated sugar	1	cup fresh or frozen cranberries (do not thaw), roughly chopped
1	tablespoon orange zest		
2	cups all-purpose flour, plus more for hands and work surface	½	cup heavy cream, plus more to brush over scones
2½	teaspoons baking powder	1	large egg
½	teaspoon salt	1½	teaspoons vanilla extract
½	cup unsalted butter, very cold		Coarse sugar to sprinkle, optional

In a large bowl, rub together sugar and orange zest. Add flour, baking powder, and salt; whisk to combine. Grate butter into flour mixture and toss to coat. Use fingers to work butter into flour until the size of small peas. Add cranberries and stir to combine. In a small bowl whisk together heavy cream, egg, and vanilla. Pour the cream mixture over flour mixture and gently mix with fork until everything is just combined. Chill for 30 minutes.

Turn dough onto lightly floured work surface. With floured hands, form into 8-inch disc, about 1 inch thick. Using a sharp knife, cut into 8 wedges. Cover and chill scones for at least 1 hour, or up to 24 hours.

Preheat oven to 400°F. Line a large baking sheet with parchment paper and arrange chilled scones 2 to 3 inches apart on sheet. Brush tops of scones with cream and sprinkle with coarse sugar. Bake for 20 to 25 minutes or until golden brown around the edges and lightly browned on top. Remove from the oven and cool. Makes 8 scones.

Overnight French Toast Casserole

- 8 to 10 cups cubed bread from one- or two-day-old French or challah bread
- 2 cups milk
- 6 large eggs
- ¼ cup packed brown sugar
- 2 teaspoons vanilla extract
- 1 teaspoon ground cinnamon
- ½ teaspoon salt

TOPPING:
- 4 tablespoons unsalted butter, melted
- ½ cup lightly packed light brown sugar
- ½ teaspoon ground cinnamon

Fresh berries, confectioner's sugar, maple syrup for serving, optional

Grease a 9 x 13-inch baking dish and spread bread cubes in dish. In a medium bowl, whisk together milk, eggs, brown sugar, vanilla, cinnamon, and salt until well combined. Pour mixture evenly over bread, then press gently with a spatula to help bread absorb the liquid. Cover dish with plastic wrap and refrigerate 8 hours or overnight. (Topping will be added next morning.)

When ready to bake, remove dish from refrigerator; preheat oven to 375°F. While oven is heating, prepare topping. In a small bowl, stir together melted butter, brown sugar, and cinnamon until smooth. Drizzle evenly over top of bread mixture.

Bake 40 to 45 minutes, until puffed and golden brown. If top is browning too quickly, loosely cover with foil for last 10 minutes. Let stand for 5 minutes before serving. Top as desired. Makes 8 to 10 servings.

Christmas and Grandmother's Kitchen

Rachel S. Fruh

No other place in all the world had the warmth and magic of Grandmother's kitchen at Christmastime. Every year on the first day of December, she tucked her plump anatomy into a wonderful, red-checked apron, and this was the signal to the whole household that, for Grandmother at least, the holiday season had officially begun. Stalwart and spunky, she was the unrivaled monarch of her domain. With a smudge of flour on her chin and wisps of stray silver curling gently about her face, she moved purposely about the room, pulling crocks of sugar from the pantry, stoking the fire, and plunging her thick, strong fists into mounds of leavened dough.

Within a few hours, the plain little kitchen with its worn wooden floors and tired old furniture was transformed into a wonderland of childhood fancies. Even the eccentric old woodstove seemed to enjoy the excitement as it popped and spit contentedly in the corner, teasing the copper teakettle into singing tenor and steaming up the lace-framed windowpanes with its hot, smoky breath. On the front lid, thick chocolate syrup bubbled merrily in an iron kettle and spit out tiny beads that sizzled and danced on the stovetop. Next to it, a cauldron of nutty caramel fudge frothed and foamed to its peak of perfection. Meanwhile, inside the oven, another wonder was being performed. Out of its mysterious depths emerged giant cookie sheets laden with golden brown cutouts, popovers, and fat, saucy gingerbread boys bulging at the seams of their imaginary blue jeans. And across the room on the sideboard, a row of glass cookie jars proudly flaunted their holiday dainties: *Pfeffer Nüsse*, *Lebkuchen*, and sugar cookies the size of Grandmother's china saucers. Out of this happy clutter ascended a wondrous concoction, a fragrant intermingling of cinnamon, yeast sponge, lemon extract, melted butter, and fresh-ground cloves that intoxicated all who breathed it with the nostalgia of the holiday season.

Even though her red-checked apron has been folded and put away for the last time, the old woodstove has forever ceased to tease the copper teakettle into singing tenor, and the cookie jars are no longer filled, the memory of Grandmother and her kitchen will always warm my heart with the magic that is Christmas.

Image © Pinkyone/Shutterstock

Holiday Aroma

Ruth H. Underhill

There's something about the kitchen
these past few busy days;
it has a special aroma,
wonderful in many ways.

It seems to be the favorite room
of everybody here;
It must be the fragrant odor
at this Christmas time of year.

See the plum pudding bubbling;
smell the sweetness of the spice.
Of all the times of all the year,
Christmastime is oh, so nice!

Over near the cozy fire,
we're busy cracking nuts;
sister hums a Christmas carol
as candied fruit she cuts.

The cookie jar is brimming;
I just went to take a peek,
but with Mother watching oh so close,
there's no chance for one to sneak.

Mother keeps opening the oven door,
popping goodies in and out;
all this can only mean one thing:
Christmas is near, without a doubt!

Image © Daniel Hurst/Stocksy

There's a Christmas Ago
Loise Pinkerton Fritz

There's a Christmas ago
    that in memory glows
like the flame of a bright, burning light.
And it shines, brightly shines,
    o'er chasms of time . . .
that beautiful Christmas of white.

I can hear sleigh bells ring . . .
    ting-a-ling, ting-a-ling,
hear that jolly old "ho, ho, ho, ho."
It resounds through the years,
    through the laughter and tears . . .
that Christmas of long, long ago.

There's a Christmas ago,
    and I treasure it so;
in my storehouse of joys, it's the crown.
For 'twas then that I heard
    of a Baby Boy's birth
in a manger in Bethlehem town.

Though time in its flight
    finds me no more a child,
still I treasure that Christmas of old.
And my heart ever yearns
    once again to return
to that Christmas of long, long ago.

Christmas Memories
Inez Franck

The happiness of Christmas lies
in memories held most dear;
remembering each loving friend,
each blessing through the year.

As holly hangs upon the door
and bells ring merrily,
may love return its golden gleam
around your Christmas tree!

TREASURED MEMORIES *by Kim Norlien. Image Kim Norlien. Courtesy of MHS Licensing.*

Christmas

Patricia Emme

As songs of Christmas fill the air,
and Christmas magic's everywhere,
may all your loved ones far and near
be blessed with Christmas love and cheer.

A Christmas Wish

Henry Van Dyke

I am thinking of you today, because it is Christmas. And I wish you joy. And tomorrow, because it is the day after Christmas, I shall wish you joy. Mayhap I cannot tell you about it from day to day, for you may be far away, or we may be entangled with the things of life. But it makes no difference—my thoughts and my wishes will be with you. Whatever of joy or success comes to you, I shall be glad. Clear through the year, without pretense, I wish you the spirit of Christmas.

Image © Marina April/Adobe Stock

Bits & Pieces

How can you make this the happiest Christmas of your life? Simply by trying to give yourself to others. Put something of yourself into everything you give. A gift, however small, speaks its own language. And when it tells of the love of the giver, it is truly blessed.
—Norman Vincent Peale

Each sight, each sound of Christmas
and fragrances sublime
make hearts and faces happy
this glorious Christmastime.
—Carice Williams

At Christmas play
and make good cheer,
for Christmas comes
but once a year.
—Thomas Tusser

May you have the greatest two gifts of all on these holidays: someone to love and someone who loves you.
—John Sinor

From home to home and heart to heart, from one place to another, the warmth and joy of Christmas brings us closer to each other.
—Emily Matthews

Dearer than memory, brighter than expectation is the ever returning *now* of Christmas. Why else, each time we greet its return, should happiness ring out in us like a peal of bells?
—Elizabeth Bowen

But peaceful was the night
wherein the Prince of Light
His reign of peace
upon the earth began.
—John Milton

The tree is full of trimmings
and gifts for girl and boy.
The world is full of
Christmas cheer;
our hearts are full of joy.
—Author Unknown

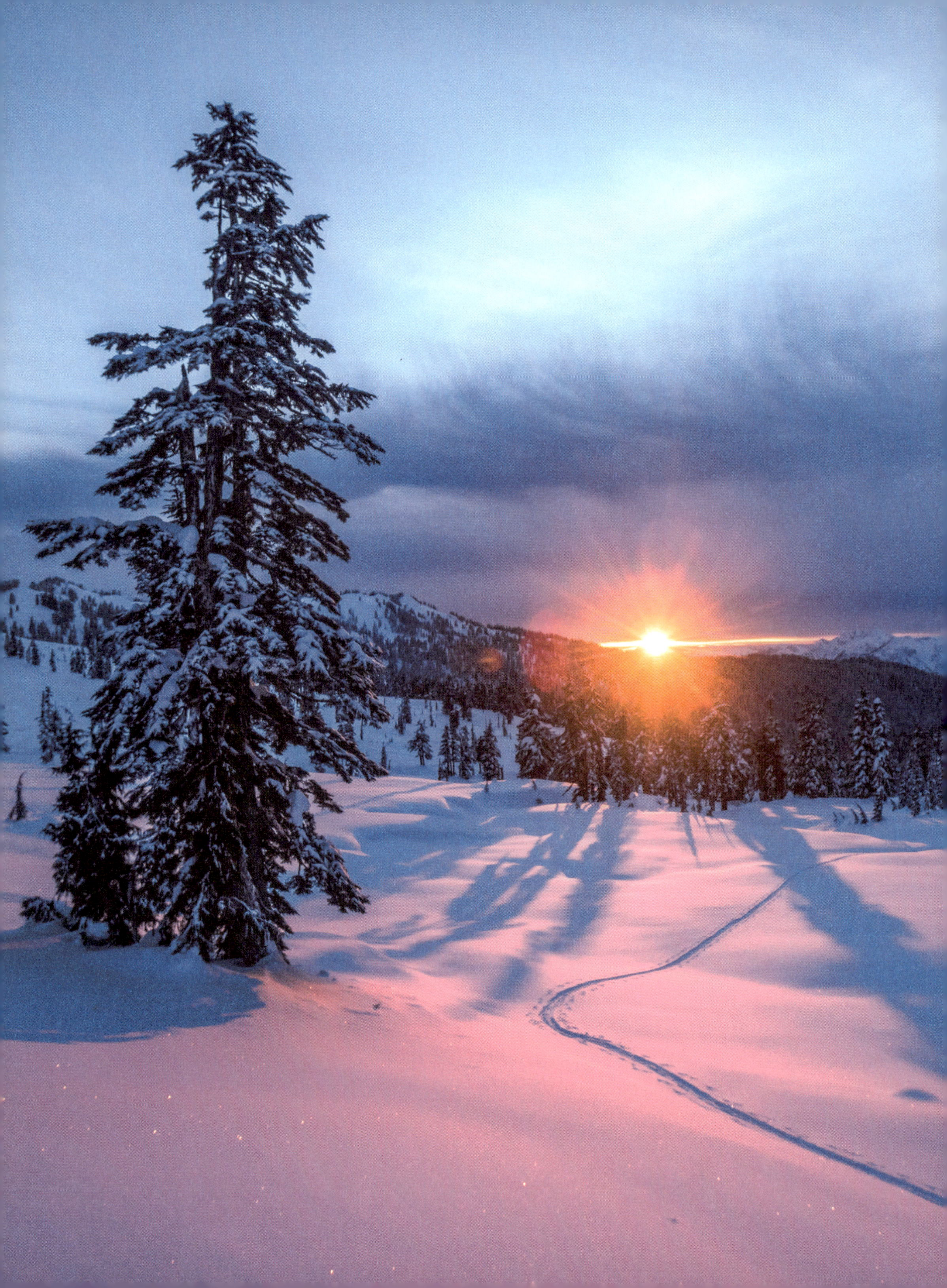

Leisure
Grace Noll Crowell

I shall attend to my little errands of love
    early this year,
So that the brief days before Christmas may be
    unhampered and clear
Of the fever of hurry. The breathless rushing
    that I have known in the past
Shall not possess me. I shall be calm in my soul
    and ready at last
For Christmas—the Mass of Christ—I shall kneel
    and call out his name;
I shall have leisure—I shall go out alone
    from my roof and my door;
I shall not miss the silver silence of stars
    as I have before;
And oh, perhaps, if I stand there very still
    and very long,
I shall hear what the clamor of living
    has kept from me—
        the angel's song.

Journey
Mary Ann Putman

Come, take my hand, dear,
  you and I will go
whispering softly
  through falling stars
    of snow.

In the wonder of
  whiteness,
innocence is young.

From the lips of children
"O Holy Night" is sung.

Shepherd bells are
  ringing
into the hushed white air.
The quiet holds a
  reverence;
love is everywhere!

Through My Window

Pop-Up Nativity

Pamela Kennedy

Having attended large churches that produce professional-quality productions each Christmas, I've become accustomed to a certain type of Nativity play. Mary, attired in a flowing azure robe meekly rides a real donkey down the center aisle. A classically trained Joseph walks beside her, occasionally offering gestures of support and encouragement. An angelic chorus breaks into four-part harmony while amazed shepherds quake as they gather up their bleating lambs for the trip to Bethlehem. Once the blessed baby arrives (a real infant, of course), the Holy Family dotes lovingly, gazing into the straw-filled manger. Then, as the orchestra modulates into a minor key, a trio of richly attired kings proceed to the scene, bearing ornate casks and boxes while a well-rehearsed choir fills the auditorium again with *glorias in excelsis deo*. The overall effect is nothing short of awe-inspiring.

If that is the Broadway of Nativity plays, what I witnessed in our smaller and more modest sanctuary this past Christmas resides at the other end of the spectrum. This "Pop-Up Nativity," was an impromptu, come-as-you-are affair open to all children brought to the Christmas Eve service by their dutiful parents (who were probably hoping to inspire their youngsters with the "real" story of Christmas before the inevitable chaos of stockings and Santa). As the families arrived, our intrepid children's director escorted the kids to a room filled with costumes from many Christmases past. Prospective shepherds dug through piles of colorful robes in a variety of sizes, swaths of striped material suitable for head coverings, and a stack of wooden crooks. Aspiring angels assessed the stash of white robes and gold tinsel halos. A junior-high boy with a good reading voice assumed the role of the angel Gabriel and two other older students were tapped to serve as Mary and Joseph. A well-loved baby doll wrapped in swaddling clothes served as Baby Jesus. In one corner, sparkling crowns and brocade were claimed by a quartet of kings—who said there could only be three? Some of the youngest participants were directed toward animal prints and fake sheep's wool with matching headgear to fill in the roles of cows and sheep. The costumed young actors then reunited with their parents in the pews until it was time for the blessed event.

There was no rehearsal, but the directions were simple: The pastor would read the story of the Nativity from the gospels of Luke and Matthew and, as the children heard the verses relating to their particular characters, they would leave their parents and come forward to create a replica of the Nativity scene around a homemade wooden manger stuffed with straw. What could go wrong?

Piano music played softly while the events of that first Christmas unfolded on the chancel. As the various characters took their places, little sheep and shepherds jostled with angels and cows for a good spot to sit. Two strong-willed shepherds fought a brief duel with their crooks before deciding who stood where. Excited angels, along with a cow or two, waved frantically to family members in the congregation. When cued by the music director, adults sang appropriate verses of familiar carols to accompany the tableau. Things seemed to be going according to plan when, about halfway through "Away in a Manger," there appeared to be a bit of a kerfuffle up front. A four-year old dressed as a sheep stealthily crept closer and closer to the Baby Jesus and, when he was finally near the manger, he reached in to rescue the holy infant from the scratchy straw. With a grin of satisfaction, he settled down, cross-legged, cradling the baby protectively. Undaunted by perturbed glances from the heavenly host, urgent gestures from Joseph, and loud whispers from the rest of his flock, the littlest lamb rocked and comforted the Lamb of God.

Image © Allison/Lightstock

It wasn't the most professional of Christmas performances, but somehow, this impromptu pageant, filled with unrehearsed players, captured something genuine. Just as I imagine things might have unfolded at that first Nativity, no one knew exactly where to stand, the participants were unsure of their roles, and folks jostled one another to get a good view. But in all of it, there was truth. A little child remained the centerpiece, captivating the imagination of all those present, and illustrating the wonder of heaven come to earth so long ago.

Word Made Flesh

John 1:1–14 NIV

In the beginning was the Word, and the Word was with God, and the Word was God. He was with God in the beginning. Through him all things were made; without him nothing was made that has been made. In him was life, and that life was the light of all mankind. The light shines in the darkness, and the darkness has not overcome it.

There was a man sent from God whose name was John. He came as a witness to testify concerning that light, so that through him all might believe. He himself was not the light; he came only as a witness to the light.

The true light that gives light to everyone was coming into the world. He was in the world, and though the world was made through him, the world did not recognize him. He came to that which was his own, but his own did not receive him. Yet to all who did receive him, to those who believed in his name, he gave the right to become children of God—children born not of natural descent, nor of human decision or a husband's will, but born of God.

The Word became flesh and made his dwelling among us. We have seen his glory, the glory of the one and only Son, who came from the Father, full of grace and truth.

MINISTRY OF JOHN THE BAPTIST. *Image* © Providence Collection/GoodSalt.

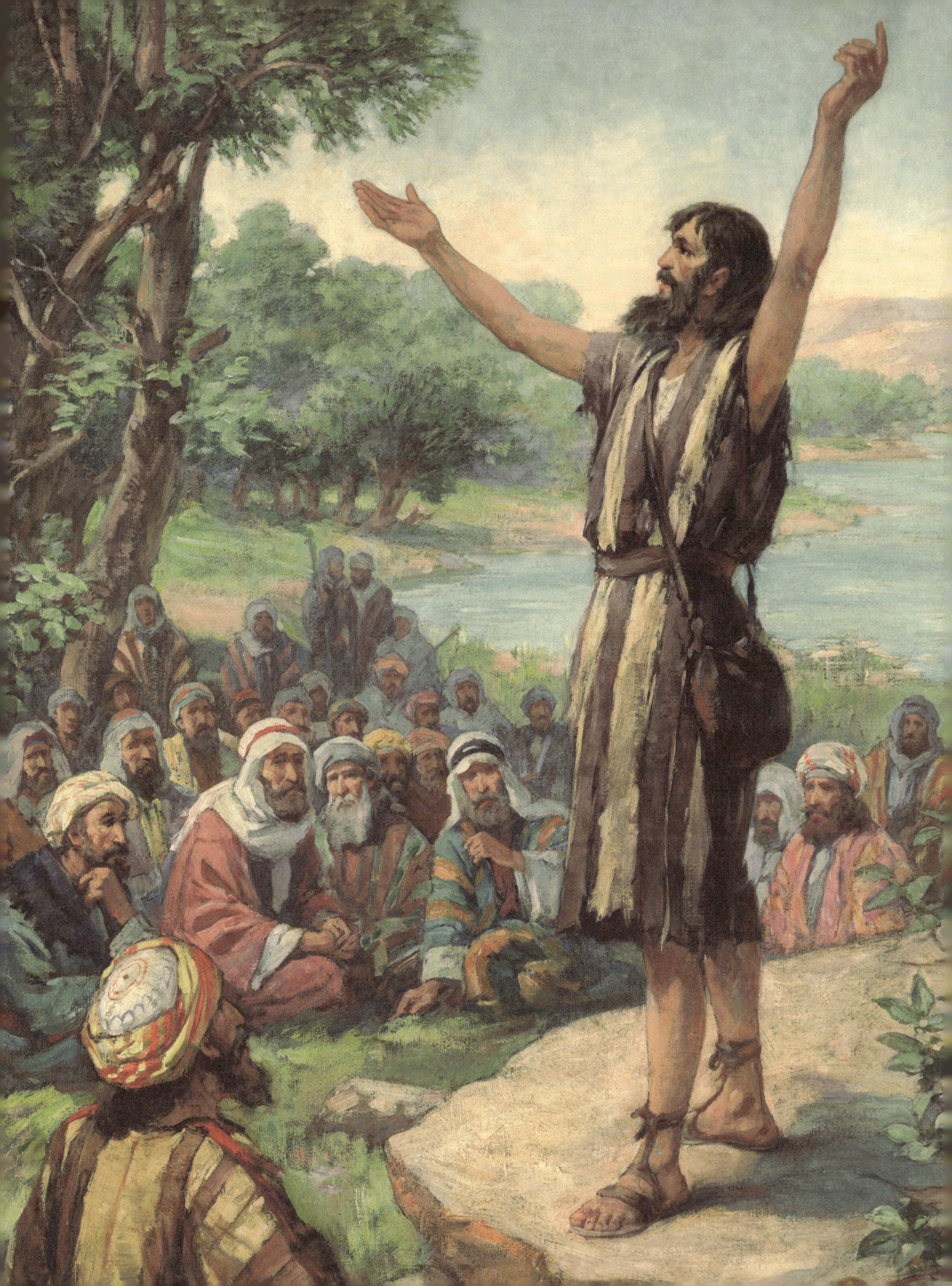

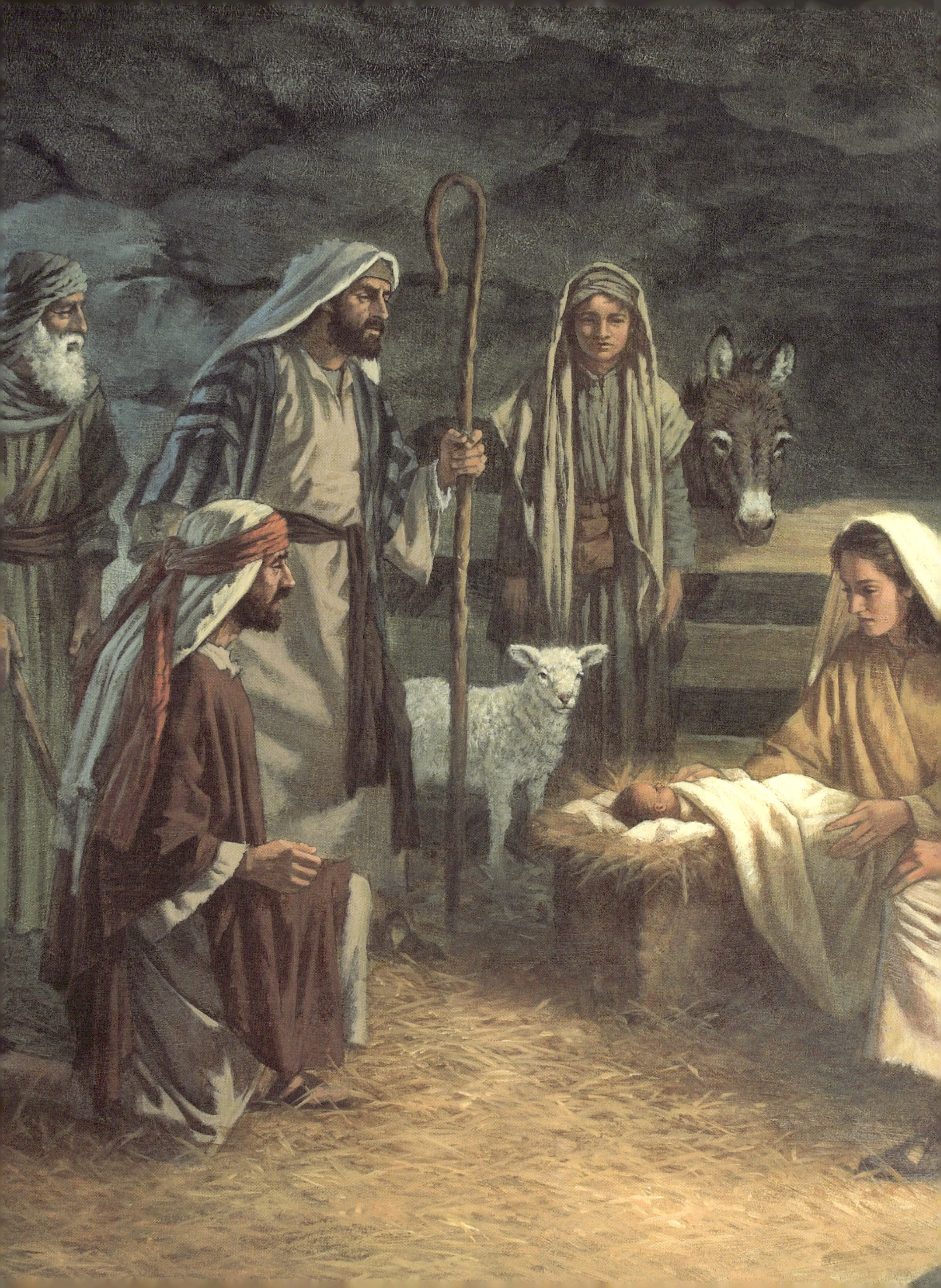

The Birth of Christ

Matthew 1:18–25 NIV

This is how the birth of Jesus the Messiah came about: His mother Mary was pledged to be married to Joseph, but before they came together, she was found to be pregnant through the Holy Spirit. Because Joseph her husband was faithful to the law, and yet did not want to expose her to public disgrace, he had in mind to divorce her quietly.

But after he had considered this, an angel of the Lord appeared to him in a dream and said, "Joseph son of David, do not be afraid to take Mary home as your wife, because what is conceived in her is from the Holy Spirit. She will give birth to a son, and you are to give him the name Jesus, because he will save his people from their sins."

All this took place to fulfill what the Lord had said through the prophet: "The virgin will conceive and give birth to a son, and they will call him Immanuel" (which means "God with us").

When Joseph woke up, he did what the angel of the Lord had commanded him and took Mary home as his wife. But he did not consummate their marriage until she gave birth to a son. And he gave him the name Jesus.

Jesus Was Born. *Image © Lifeway Collection/GoodSalt.*

THE WISE MEN AND THE STAR

Matthew 2:1–11 NIV

After Jesus was born in Bethlehem in Judea, during the time of King Herod, Magi from the east came to Jerusalem and asked, "Where is the one who has been born king of the Jews? We saw his star when it rose and have come to worship him."

When King Herod heard this he was disturbed, and all Jerusalem with him. When he had called together all the people's chief priests and teachers of the law, he asked them where the Messiah was to be born. "In Bethlehem in Judea," they replied, "for this is what the prophet has written:

> "'But you, Bethlehem, in the land of Judah,
>   are by no means least among the
>   rulers of Judah;
> for out of you will come a ruler
>   who will shepherd my people Israel.'"

Then Herod called the Magi secretly and found out from them the exact time the star had appeared. He sent them to Bethlehem and said, "Go and search carefully for the child. As soon as you find him, report to me, so that I too may go and worship him."

After they had heard the king, they went on their way, and the star they had seen when it rose went ahead of them until it stopped over the place where the child was. When they saw the star, they were overjoyed. On coming to the house, they saw the child with his mother Mary, and they bowed down and worshiped him. Then they opened their treasures and presented him with gifts of gold, frankincense and myrrh.

JOURNEY OF THE MAGI. *Image* © Corbert Gauthier. Courtesy of MHS Licensing.

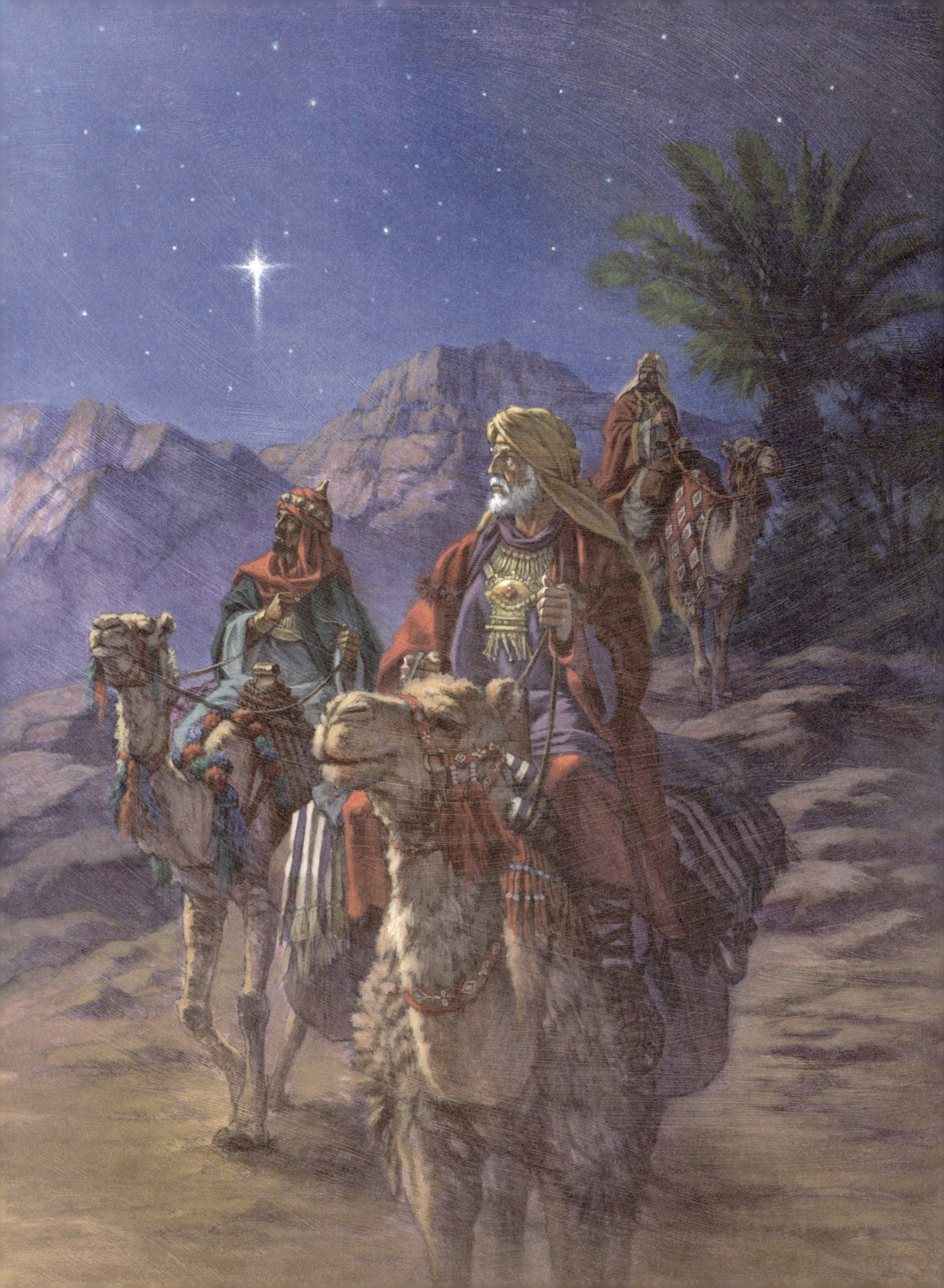

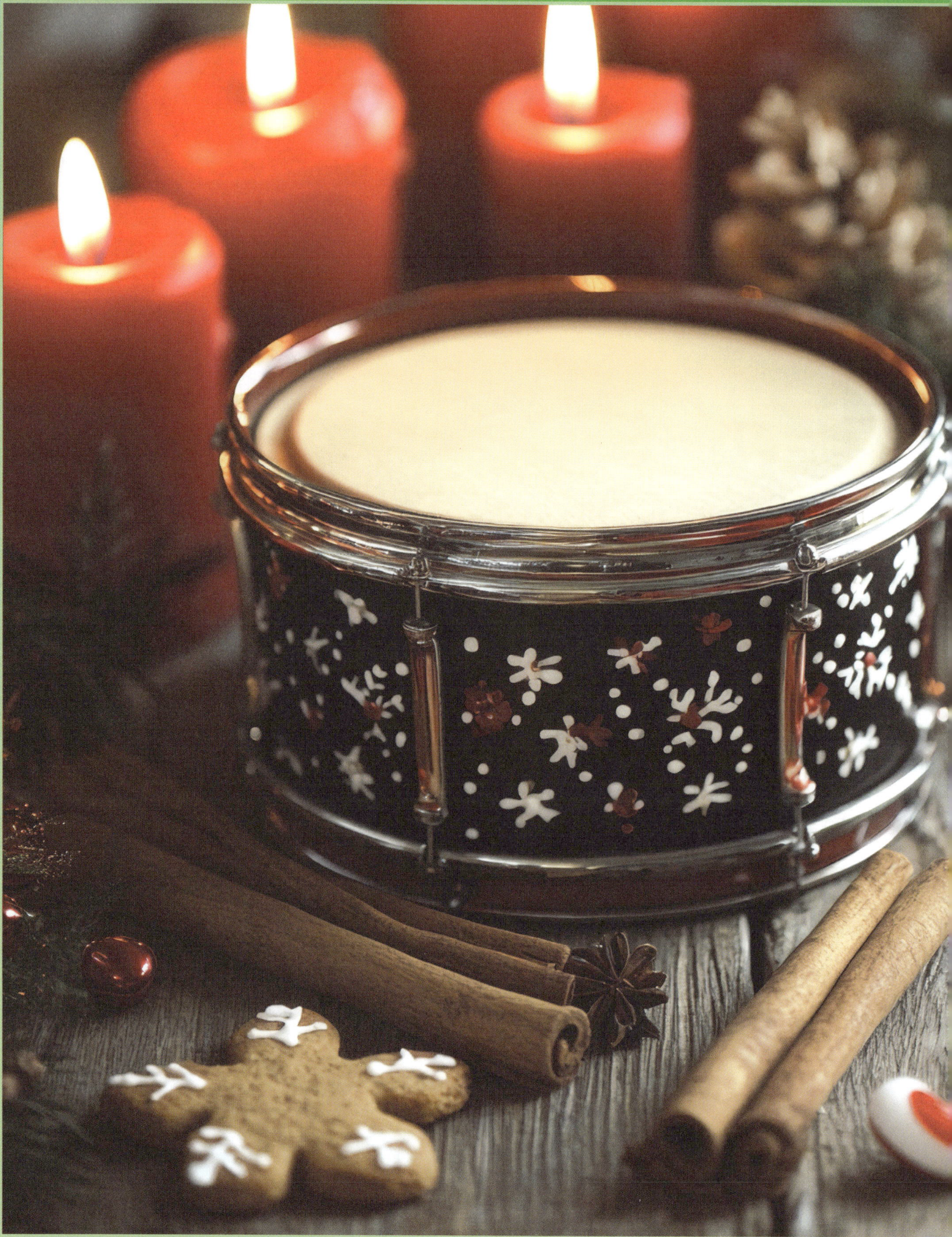

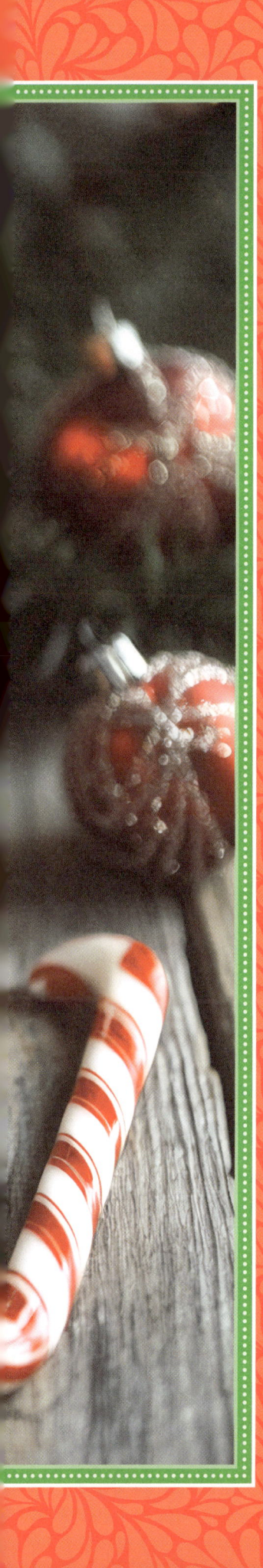

Dear Drummer Boy
Sandra Lytle

O precious little drummer boy,
I often think of you.
For on that special, holy night
you played a tune or two

in honor of the newborn King
Who in a manger lay.
You gave the only gift you had,
your deep love to convey.

Did ox and lamb and donkey too
join in for harmony,
or did they gaze in silent awe
of such a sight to see?

Oh, surely baby Jesus slept
more peacefully that night
as music serenaded Him,
and stars bathed Him in light.

Your gift—more sweet than frankincense
or myrrh or gleaming gold—
was music that welled up inside,
more than your heart could hold.

At times in life, we think our gifts
unworthy since they're small,
but God knows when we sacrifice
and give to Him our all.

Image © Megavectors/Dreamstime.com

A Little Child
Lorna Volk

A little Child
    once laid His head
upon a humble,
    holy bed
and dreamt sweet dreams
    of peace and love
while angels guarded
    from above
and sang their softest
    lullaby
to sooth Him so
    He should not cry.
And that small Child
    is still at rest
in every heart
    in every breast
of every man
    upon the earth
who celebrates
    this Baby's birth!

Sing a Song of Christmas
Lola Neff Merritt

Sing a song of Christmas;
Sweet carols fill the air.
Open up your heart with love
and drop life's daily cares.

Joyously lift up songs of praise
to our Heavenly Father above;
Who gave life's greatest gift of all,
His Son, Who came in love.

Image © Alan Lathwell/Advocate Art

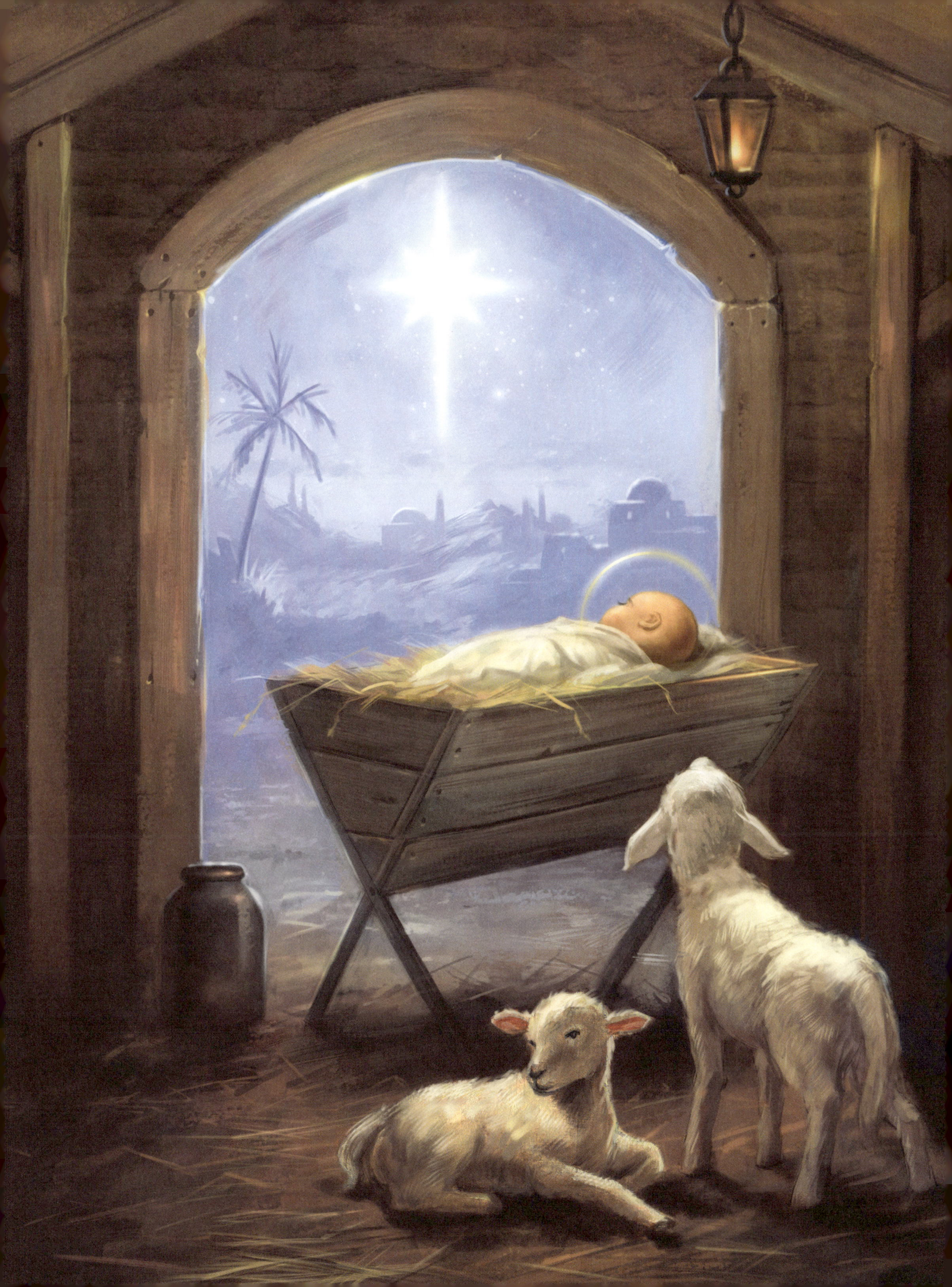

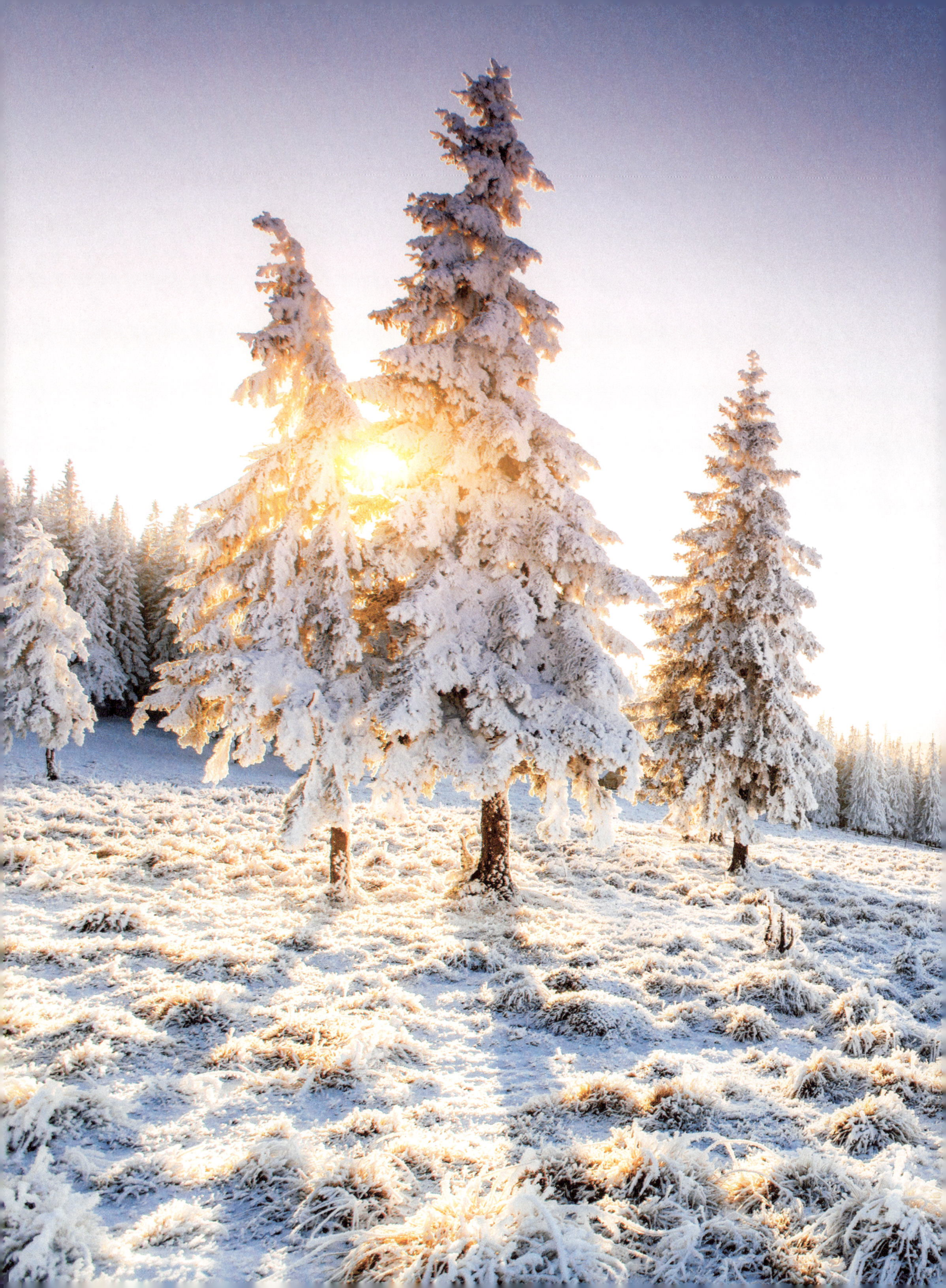

A Prayer for December
Glenda Collins Inman

Lord, help us in the days ahead,
as we celebrate Your birth,
to filter out the lesser things
and choose the things of worth.
To fix our hearts and minds on You;
our busyness to cease,
that You may work Your will in us,
and fill us with Your peace.

Were Earth a Thousand Times as Fair
Martin Luther

Were earth a thousand times as fair,
Beset with gold and jewels rare,
She yet were far too poor to be
A narrow cradle, Lord, for Thee.

The Voice of the Christ Child
Phillips Brooks

The earth has grown cold with its burden of care,
But at Christmas it always is young.
The heart of the jewel burns lustrous and fair,
And its soul full of music breaks forth on the air
When the song of the Angels is sung.
It is coming, old earth, it is coming tonight;
On the snowflakes which cover thy sod,
The feet of the Christ-child fall gently and white,
And the voice of the Christ-child
   tells out with delight
That mankind are the children of God.

Image © standret/iStock

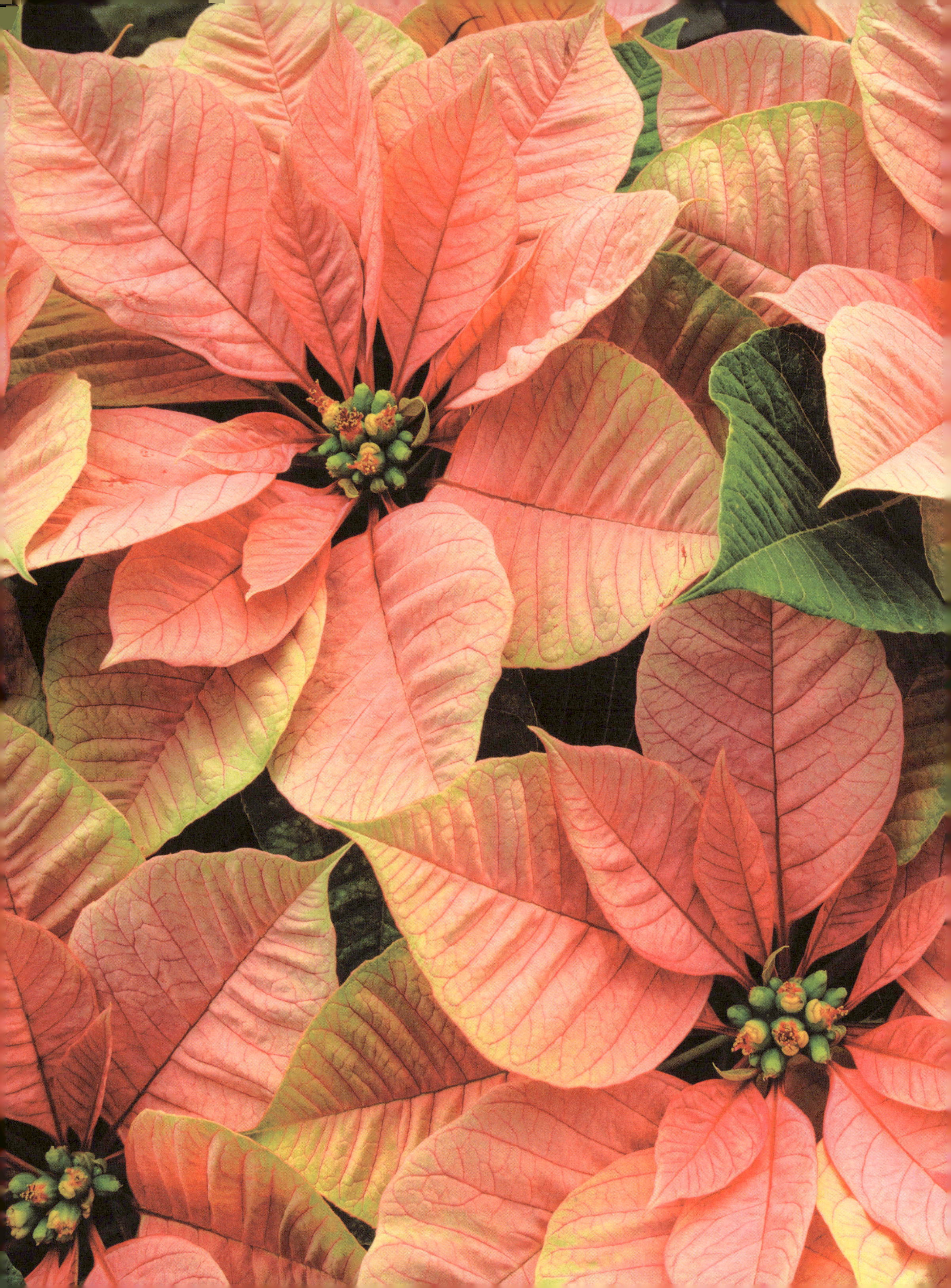

It's Not About the Gifts

Clay Harrison

It's not about the gifts we give
    or gifts that we receive.
It's about the way we live,
    how deeply we believe.
There are no frosty snowmen,
    no reindeer flying high,
but the star above Christ's manger
    still shines brightly in the sky.

It's not about a tinseled tree,
    a decorated door;
it's about the joy within us
    when we worship and adore.
It's about the Christmas carols
    that set our hearts aglow,
the hugs we share with loved ones
    beneath the mistletoe.

It's about things we share with others,
    the web of love we weave.
It's not about the gifts we give
    or gifts that we receive.

Image © zigzagmtart/Adobestock

In a Little Town
Geo. L. Ehrman

We saw a lovely little church,
its steeple all aglow,
in a little country town
where roofs were thatched
    with snow!

The friendly folk were all around
and music filled the air,
for roaming carolers strolled about
their Christmas songs to share!

As we drove on through
    snow-clad hills
to meet our loved ones too,
the reverence for Jesus' birth
filled our hearts anew!

Promise
Gloria R. Milbrath

Long centuries past,
a promise was made
that Jesus, the Savior,
would come as a babe.

And so it all happened
one deep, starlit night.
The Promise was born—
the true Christmas light.

Hope Runs Deep.
Image © Chuck Pinson.

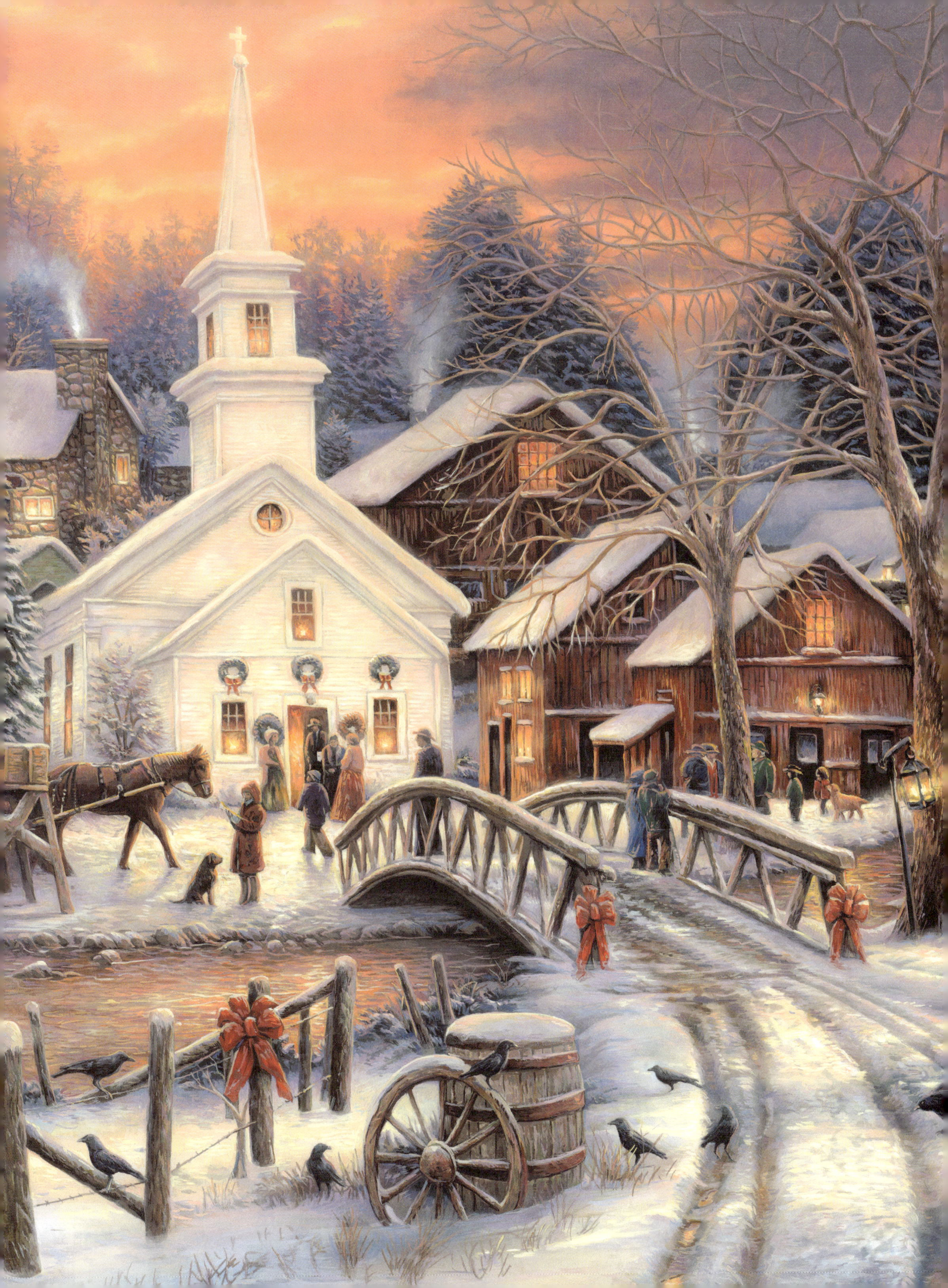

Happy Christmastide
Minnie Klemme

The fallow fields are white with snow;
the lakes are frozen glass.
And if you listen you may hear
the Christmas season pass.

The sleighbells ring along the roads;
from sleds and cutters too.
The air is filled with happy shouts
as friends greet old and new.
Piled high with gifts and trees,
the shoppers hurry home,
while carols ring from house to house,
from window, door, and dome.

We light again the Advent wreath;
invite the Christ inside.
And share again with one and all
the happy Christmastide.

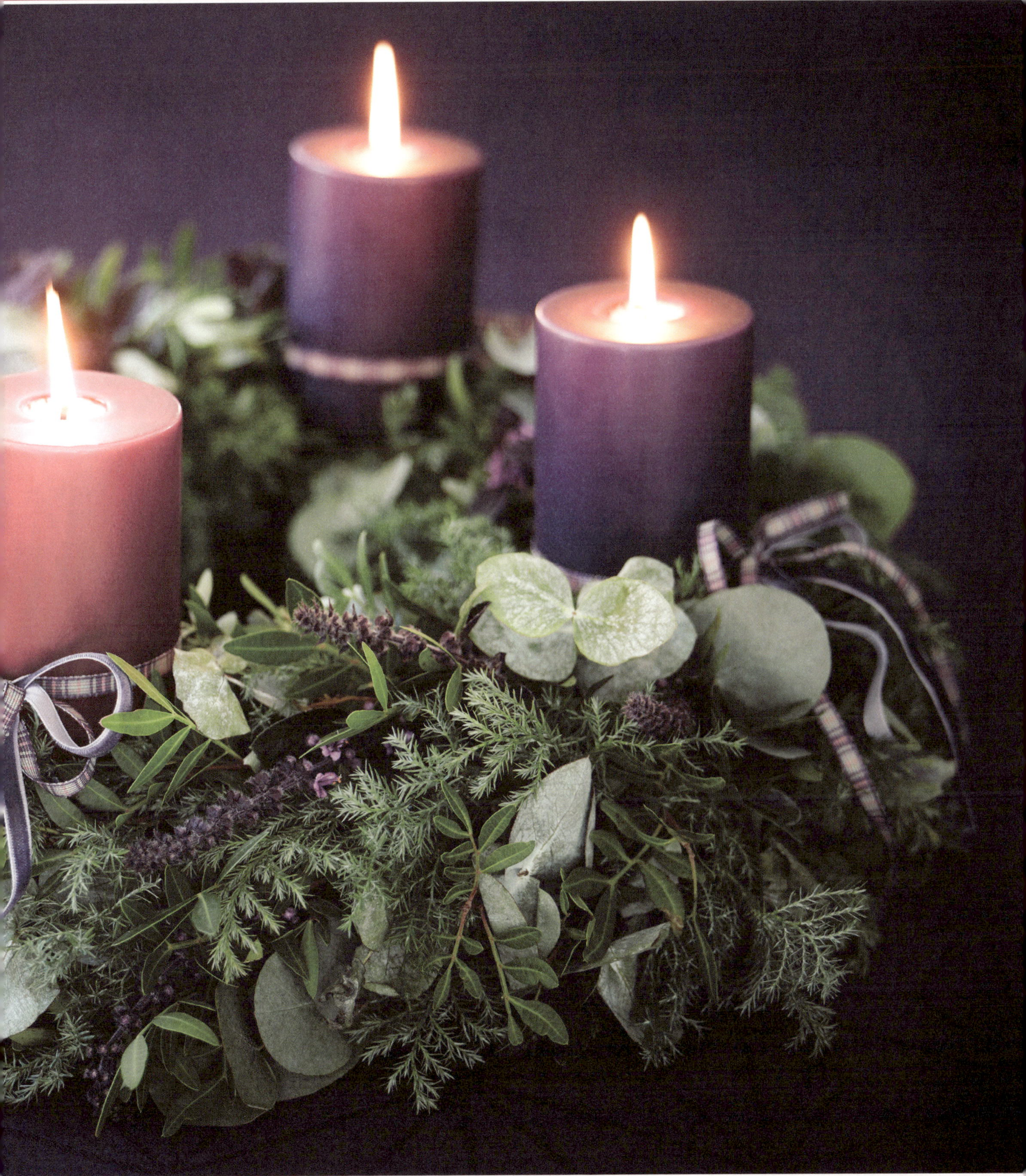

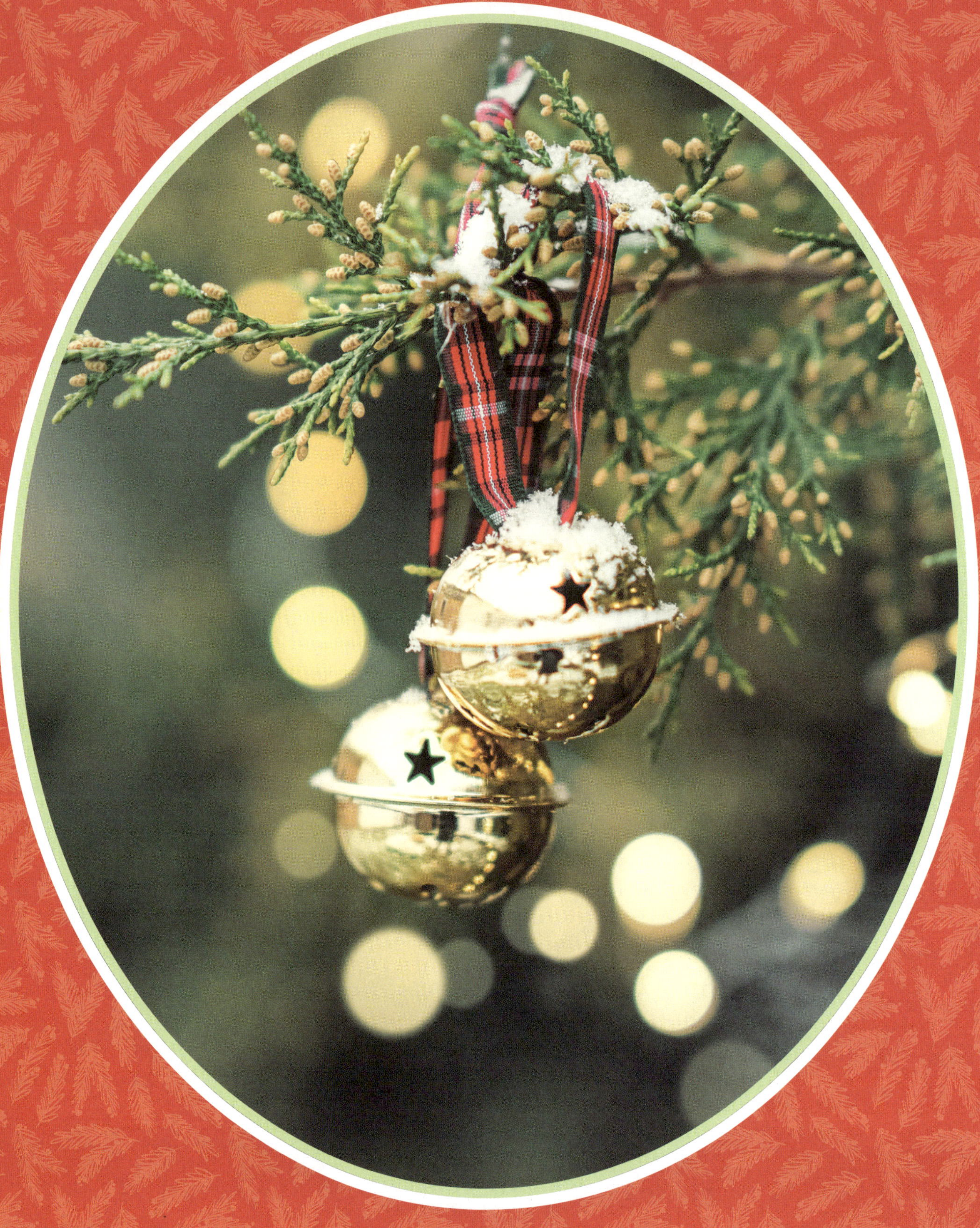

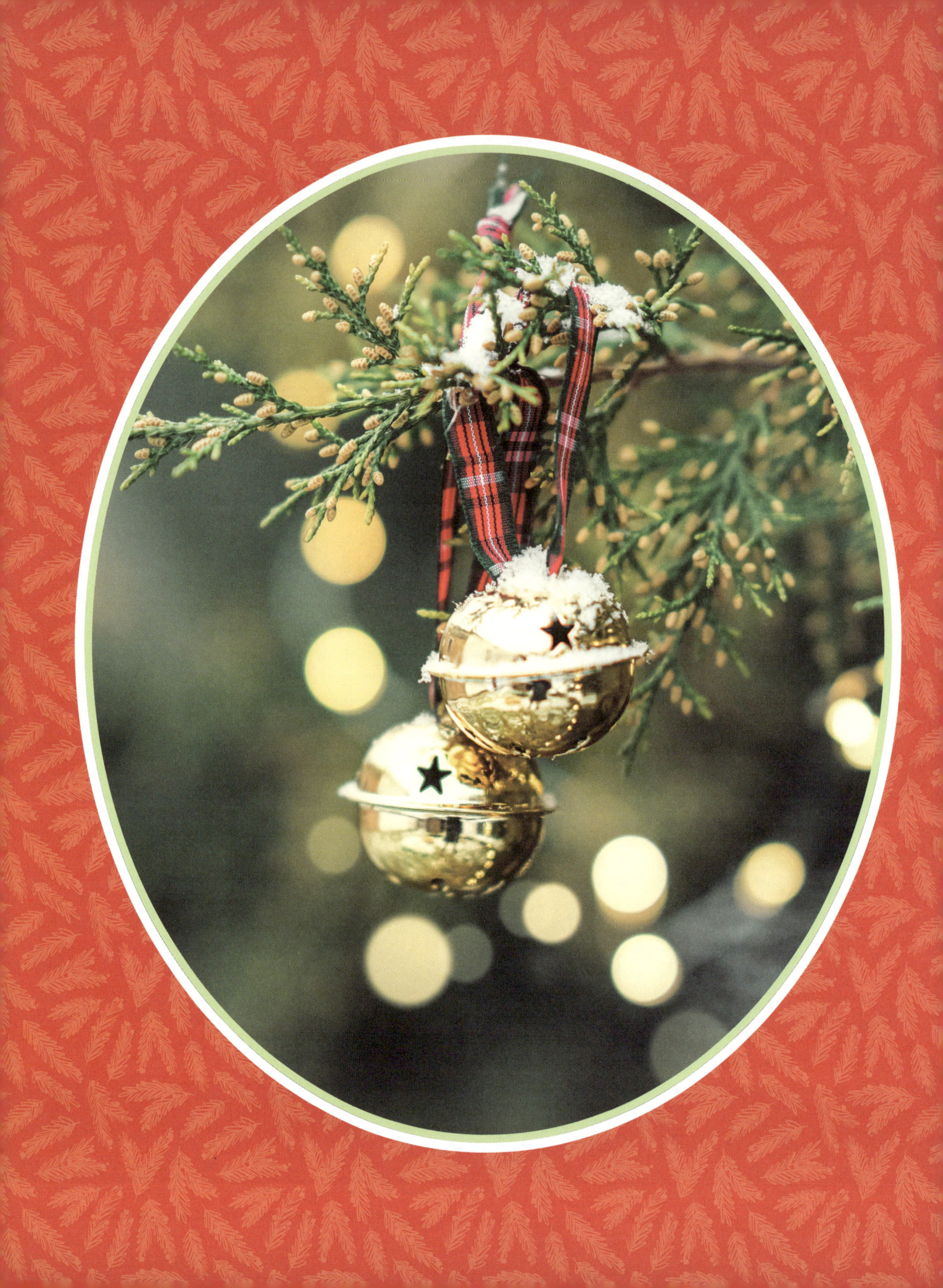

Ring On, O Happy Bells
Joy Belle Burgess

Ring on, O bells of gladness,
with your message of good cheer;
peal forth the merry tidings
in cadence sweet and clear.

Chime forth your skyborne music,
with its intervals of mirth;
arouse the aspirations
and hopes of all the earth.

Ring on, O bells of gladness,
with the joy you now impart;
ring on and on, O happy bells,
and bring a song to every heart.

The Bells
Edgar Allen Poe

Hear the sledges with the bells,
Silver bells!
What a world of merriment their
　　melody foretells!
How they tinkle, tinkle, tinkle,
In the icy air of night!
While the stars, that oversprinkle
All the heavens, seem to twinkle
With a crystalline delight;
Keeping time, time, time,
In a sort of Runic rhyme,
To the tintinnabulation
　　that so musically wells
From the bells, bells, bells, bells,
Bells, bells, bells—
From the jingling and the
　　tinkling of the bells.

Image © Natalia Shmatova/Shutterstock

I Didn't Miss the Joy!
Donna Miesbach

The celebration's over now,
the day has come and gone.
Shepherds, wise men, tales of old,
all memories drawn upon.

I wasn't at the stable.
I didn't see the Boy.
But thanks to God's all-gracing love,
I didn't miss the joy!

I didn't miss the glowing hearts,
the music in the air,
the love and peace that overflowed
from glad hearts everywhere.

The tree lies barren in the snow.
The gifts are put away.
Yet in the silent aftermath
my heart still wants to pray.

For while I wasn't there to kneel
in wonder at the Boy,
thanks to God's unending love
I didn't miss the joy!

Image © Lucky Business/Shutterstock

New Year Prayer
Rhonda Reed

I thank You, Lord, for this new year—
For every joy, for every task, for every tear,
For every lesson learned, for every promise true,
For comfort, for correction that leads my heart to You.

As I rejoice in everything that comes my earthly way,
I find Your heavenly purpose as I study, praise, and pray.
The years are but a journey, your example is my guide.
With this new year before me, Lord, help me stay
    close by Your side.

ISBN-13: 978-1-5460-0869-9

Published by Ideals
Hachette Book Group
1290 Avenue of the Americas
New York, NY 10104

Copyright © 2025 by Hachette Book Group, Inc.
All rights reserved. No part of this publication may be reproduced or transmitted in any form or by any means, electronic or mechanical, including photocopy, recording, or any information storage and retrieval system, without permission in writing from the publisher.

Printed and bound in Canada

Publisher, Peggy Schaefer
Editor, Rebekah Moredock
Designer and Photo Research, Marisa Jackson
Proofreader, Kate Etue

Cover: Image © Clive Nichols/GAP Interiors
Inside front cover art © Anastasiia/Adobe Stock and Anlomaja/Adobe Stock (montage). Inside back cover art © Minpin/Dreamstime.

Join a community of *Ideals* readers on Facebook at: www.facebook.com/IdealsMagazine
Readers are invited to submit original poetry and prose for possible use in future publications. Please send no more than four typed submissions to: Hachette Book Group, Attn: *Ideals* Submissions, 830 Crescent Centre Dr., Suite 450, Franklin, Tennessee 37067. Editors cannot guarantee your material will be used, but we will contact you if we do wish to publish.

Acknowledgments

"Christmas Is a Season for Giving" by Helen Steiner Rice, © 1987 Cincinnati Museum Center. Reprinted with permission of the Cincinnati Museum Center.

OUR THANKS to the following authors or their heirs: June Masters Bacher, Deborah A. Bennett, Anne Kennedy Brady, Loretta Bauer Buckley, Joy Belle Burgess, Eileen Burnett, Louise Pugh Corder, Grace Noll Crowell, Tracy Crump, Geo L. Ehrman, Patricia Emme, Inez Franck, Loise Pinkerton Fritz, Rachel S. Fruh, J. Harold Gwynne, Clay Harrison, Glenda Collins Inman, Pamela Kennedy, Marguerite Kingman, Minnie Klemme, Andrew L. Luna, Sandra Lytle, Lola Neff Merritt, Donna Miesbach, Gloria R. Milbrath, Virginia Blanck Moore, Rebekah Moredock, Mary Ann Putman, Rhonda Reed, Eileen Spinelli, Ruth H. Underhill, Lorna Volk, Lois Anne Williams, Ruth C. Wintle.

Scripture quotations, unless otherwise indicated, are taken from *The Holy Bible*, New International Version®, NIV®. Copyright © 1973, 1978, 1984, 2011 by Biblica, Inc. Used with permission of Zondervan. All rights reserved worldwide. www.zondervan.com

Every effort has been made to establish ownership and use of each selection in this book. If contacted, the publisher will be pleased to rectify any inadvertent errors or omissions in subsequent editions.